I0617301

PLEZE RAYBON

UNDERSTANDING IS THE KEY

THE TRUTH

VOL. 2

Understanding is the Key: The Truth Vol. 2

© 2025 by Pleze Raybon
Published in the United States of America

ISBN Paperback: 9798992639803
ISBN EBOOK: 9798992639810

Table of Contents

INTRODUCTION

There's a minor but unruly member among our body parts: the Tongue: **James 3:1-12**, verses one through twelve. James warms leaders, saying they are held to a higher standard. But the primary focus is on the power of the Tongue.

Verse one: Not many should become teachers, my brothers, (Why)? Because you know that we will receive a stricter judgment. Verse two: For we all stumble in many ways. If anyone does not stumble in what he says, he is mature, and able also to control the whole body. Verse three: If we put pits into the mouths of horses so they obey us, we direct their entire bodies. Verse four: And consider ships: Though very large and driven by fierce winds, they are guided by a tiny rudder wherever the will of the pilot directs. Verse five: (Here, we will see the main character and its potential). So, too, though the Tongue is a small part of the body, it boasts great things. Consider how a small fire sets ablaze in a large forest. Verse six: And the Tongue is a fire. The Tongue, a world of unrighteousness, is placed among our members. It stains the whole body, sets the course of life on fire, and is itself set on fire by hell. Verse seven: Every kind of animal, bird, reptile, and fish is tamed and has been tamed by humankind; Verse eight: but no one can tame the Tongue. It is a restless evil, full of deadly poison. Verse nine: With the Tongue, we bless our Lord and Father, and with it, we curse people who are made in God's likeness. Verse ten: Blessing and curing come out of the same mouth. My brothers and sisters, these things should not be this way. Verse eleven: (Question) Does a spring pour sweet and bitter water from the same opening? (NO!) Verse twelve: Can a fig tree produce olives, my brothers and sisters, or a grapevine produce figs? (NO!) Neither can a saltwater spring yield fresh water.

THE POWER OF WORDS

Let's start with the definition of words: sounds or a combination of sounds having meaning and forming an indivisible linguistic unit. Words can produce Faith or Fear, transform, or conform. When used correctly, they can be a light. When misused, they can be a snare to your Soul.

As a child, I didn't understand why there was so much hatred and injustice in our world. As I advanced, I realized that the Tongue of man has caused all this chaos and mischief.

When I began to study God's word, it became more apparent. I understand that a guileful heart makes a guileful Tongue. **Matt. 12:34** says, "Out of the abundance of the heart, the mouth speaks." (Here is a Quote): "A fool's heart is in his Tongue, but a wise man's Tongue is in his heart."

Jesus said, A good man brings good things out of the good stored up in his heart, and an evil man brings evil things out of the evil stored up in his heart, (**Luke 6:45**). Because out of the abundance of the heart, the mouth speaks!

Father, in the name of Jesus, I pray for the readers of this book (Myself included). I pray that we realize the power of this unruly member in our mouths - the Tongue. But again, it can be a light, or it can be a snare!

Proverbs 18:21 says, "Death and life are in the power of the Tongue." when I hear people quoting that verse, they always say life and death are in the power of the Tongue. But as you can see in scripture. It's "death and life are in the power of the Tongue". Why is that so significant? (I'm sure Brother Solomon had his reasons for phrasing it that way). But look at it from this point of view: we were born in sin and death. That was our state of mind! Consciously and unconsciously, we spoke of death and destruction because that was our fate!

Therefore, we need the enlightenment of God's word because His word is **LIFE!**

Jesus said in St. John 6:63, "It is the Spirit who gives life, the flesh profits nothing. The words that I speak to you are Spirit, and they are life". We are transformed from glory to glory by this living word; it can transform us into the image of Christ. 2nd Cor. 3:18 (CSB) says, "We all, with unveiled faces, are looking as in a mirror at the glory of the Lord and are being transformed into the same image from glory to glory; this is from the Lord who is the Spirit." (Did you get that)? We are transformed into His image by beholding His glory through prayer, studying, and obeying His living word.

We strive for that because **Prov.** 18:21 emphasizes that our words can have a profound impact, either for good or ill.

So, we must be mindful of the words we choose and their potential consequences. Jesus said in Matt. 12:36-37 "That every careless word will be judged, and that our words will either acquit or condemn us."

Matt. 15:11,18 Jesus said, "It's not what goes into the mouth that defiles a person, but what comes out of it. (Reflecting the state of the heart).

Eph. 4:29 urges believers to speak helpful and edifying words rather than harmful or destructive words. Prov. 12:18 (NIV) "The words of the reckless pierce like swords, but the Tongue of the wise brings healing."

Prov. 15:4: "A gentle Tongue is a tree of life, but perverseness in it breaks the Spirit." (That is why we are admonished to put away anger). Eph. 4:29-32 Let no evil talk come out of your mouths, but only such as is good for edifying as fits the occasion that it may impart grace to those who hear. 30.

And do not grieve the Holy Spirit of God in whom you were sealed for the day of redemption. Ver. 31 Tells us to put away all bitterness, anger, harsh words, and malicious behavior, as well as engaging in immoral lifestyles or having impure thoughts. Prov. 16:12 Whoever is slow to anger is better than the mighty, and he who rules his Spirit than he who takes a city. (I will leave you with this thought)! James 1:26 If you claim to be religious but don't control your Tongue, you are fooling yourself, and your religion is worthless.

THE PURIFYING OF THE SOUL

Gal. 5:17 reveals that the Spirit and the Flesh contradict one another. (Question) Why are they at odds? (Answer) The Soul animates the body, giving it movement or expression. The battle is for the Soul! (Why)? Because the Soul will express the activities of the flesh or the activities of the Spirit. But the goal of a believer is to align himself with the Fruit of the Spirit. So, we are told to renew the mind, so that we may prove what is the good, and acceptable, and perfect will of God is, **Romans 12:2.** Also, in **First Peter, 1:22,** The Soul is purified by obeying the truth through the Spirit.

With that in mind, let's look at some scriptures that reveal the detriment of the Soul led by the flesh. **Prov. 18:7** says, "A fool's mouth is his destruction, and his lips are a snare of his Soul."

The word destruction means dissolution, which means the act of dissolving; it also implies consternation, which means dismay or amazement, leading to confusion or fear. (Think about that) The fool's mouth is the cause of his dissolving or breakdown.

They (The fools) are snared and entrapped by their own words. And they are easily influenced by demon Spirits. So, instead of building up, they destroy; instead of speaking of life, they speak of death. They are capable of destroying everything in their path. **Prov. 24:1-2** tells us not to be envious of evil people and not desire to be with them. (Here's why)!

Because their heart studies destruction, and their lips talk of mischief.

The breakdown or dissolving begins with the individuals. The venom that comes from their mouths defiles them. They don't love themselves or anyone else. Their actions are perpetrated by their words.

A few contrasts will give us a better understanding. **Prov. 29:8** says, "Scornful men bring a city into a snare, but wise men turn away the Wrath of God." **(Jesus came to deliver us from the Wrath of God).** The word scornful means derision, contempt, ridicule, or mockery. That's what brings a city into a snare. But we who are born again understand the power of prayer.

Prov. 11:11 says, "By the blessings of the upright, the city is exalted. We bless the city by praying, interceding, and casting down everything that exalts itself against the knowledge of God" (**2nd Cor. 10:5**). The word of God with action and prayer with action is all we need to eradicate Satan's plans in this present age. (Please understand this! The spoken prophecies will be fulfilled.)

At some point, we're all going to suffer! **2nd Timothy 2:11** confirms it; the saying is sure: "If we die with him, we shall also live with Him; if we suffer with Him, we shall also reign with Him. If we deny Him, He will deny us; if we are faithless, He remains faithful (Why)? Because He cannot deny Himself. But many of God's people are not ready for what Satan is trying to do. His main Objective is to get the Church out of the way!

2nd Thessalonians 2 reveals something noteworthy. Before the Lord returns, there will be a great falling away first. But what will cause the falling away? **(SUFFERING)!** We must understand that Satan is the god of the world. He (Satan) will cause so much suffering, and those who don't know Him will be thinking or saying: If God is real, he won't allow all of this hardship. Suffering can and will test the validity of a person's faith. It will reveal the fragility and lead to disillusionment and, eventually, abandonment.

When faced with intense suffering, it can be challenging to maintain a long-term perspective and trust that God's plan is ultimately good. The immediate pain can overshadow the hope of future glory.

This is what we (The Church) will be faced with: Matt. 24:24 "For false Christs and false Prophets will arise and will do great miracles and wonders, insomuch that if it were possible, the very elect should be deceived.

Understand this also: If you know Him, suffering can strengthen your faith. This is why we are told to learn from Him. You must know and experience Him! (I'm not trying to sound deep). But He has revealed Himself to me in a way that is undeniable. **Here is my point!** There will be a lot of suffering. If you don't know Him as you Rock, you will run to what appears to bring comfort. But there is no comfort outside of Him.

I'm going back to The power of words, and I want you to see the ultimate power of your words. **Matt. 12:37** says, "By **your** words, you will be justified, and by **your** words you will be condemned." See! **Your** words lead to actions. They can change the course of your life and others. So, let **your** words bring you into the Kingdom of God by confessing that you believe in the Lord Jesus Christ! **Romans 10:10** says, "With the heart, man believes unto righteousness, (don't miss the 'B' part of this verse). It says, "With the mouth, confession is made unto Salvation. Your words have the power to change your final destination. Words are the ultimate power given to us by God. They reveal choices!

IT WAS WRITTEN FOR OUR LEARNING

Romans 15:4 says, "Whatever was written in the past was written for our instruction or learning. So that we may have hope through endurance and through the encouragement from the scriptures."(CSB)

I will open with **Ephesians 6:12**, "For we wrestle not against flesh and blood, but against Principalities, (angelic powers, invisible powers) against the rulers of the darkness of this world, against spiritual wickedness."

We're going to look at the Testimony of an individual named Asaph. He reveals what almost happened to him. However, he didn't understand what was happening to him While under the influence of a seducing Spirit.

Who was Asaph? He was a musician whom David appointed to oversee the music for worship. He singed for the dedication of Solomon's temple (**2nd Chronicles 5:12**). He was also a seer in David's court and the son of Berachiah of the tribe of Levi. This happens a lot in the Church. If an individual is gifted, he's given a place of respect. Many of them are like Asaph, who lacked understanding. He didn't realize a seducing spirit was trying to capture him.

Eccl. 1:9 says, "That which has been is that which will be [again], and that which has been done is that which will be done again. There is nothing new under the sun. You're going to see the relevancy of this Psalm.

We know the term Hip-Hop didn't exist back then, but it is the same Spirit. Nor did the term prosperity teachers exist. But both are described perfectly in his Testimony. I read Jeremiah 10 one morning; he wrote something in **Verse 23** after comparing and placing God above Idols or anything man produces. He said, "I know, oh Lord, that the **way** of man is not in himself, that it is not in man who walks to direct his steps.

That statement was confusing until the Spirit of God gave an understanding of **Ephesians 2:1-3**. Read it, and you will understand that you are **following** the course of this world, but you are not directing your ways. If we are not led by the Spirit of God, we are led by a seducing Spirit. What is a seducing Spirit? It's a Spirit that seeks to lure or persuade individuals away from Faith and Truth, often leading them to embrace deception and evil doctrines.

These Spirits are portrayed as subtle and manipulative. These Spirits are so crafty they can take the [Written] word of God and twist it to achieve their evil agenda. Let's look at his Testimony.

Psalm 73, Brother Asaph: He's showing us the power of a seducing Spirit. What almost happened to Asaph is happening to thousands of young men and women. Asaph was very active in the Church and knew about God's goodness.

In **Verse one**, He says, "Truly God is good to the upright, to those who are pure in heart." Then, in **verse two** (You can see that he is now under attack by a seducing Spirit). "But as for me, my feet had almost stumbled, my steps had well nigh slipped." **Verse three** (Reveals what caused him almost to stumble. Look where his focus was.) "For I was envious of the arrogant, when I saw the prosperity of the wicked." (He's giving heed to a seducing Spirit. In verse four, we'll see how deceived he was!) But first, let's look at **Malachi 3:13-15** This reveals our Heavenly Father's sovereignty: He sees, knows, and hears everything! **Verse 13,** "Your words have been harsh against me," says the Lord. But you say, 'What have we spoken against you? **14.** You have said, 'It is vain to serve God. What profit is it if we keep His ordinances and walk around like mourners before the Lord of hosts? **15.** So now we call the arrogant blessed. Evil doers are exalted and prosper; when they test God, they escape [unpunished]. (That's how it looks, but you get away with nothing)! Returning to Psalm 73, **Verse four**: "For there are no pains in their death; their bodies are sound and sleek. V**erse five:** "They are not in trouble as other men are; they are not stricken like other men." (I'm amazed at how the Spirit of God pinpointed these characters). **Verse six:** "Therefore pride is their necklace; violence covers them as a garment." (Look at the necklaces these guys are wearing and the perversion). They're wearing necklaces that cost thousands of dollars, with a cross representing Christ. Then, the adversary will use them to seduce others who are Spiritually bankrupt. He said violence covers them like a garment. Look at the violence in the Hip-Hop community. (There's nothing new under the sun. **Eccles. 1:9**)

Verse seven says, "Their eyes bulge out with fatness, [they have more than the heart desires]; The imaginations of their mind run riot [with foolishness]. (This individual has over one hundred cars; that's foolish)! **Verse eight:** "They speak loftily with malice or with the intent to do evil. **Verse nine** reminds me of the prosperity teachers. It says, "They set their mouths against Heaven, and their tongues strut across the earth. (**They set their mouths against Heaven)!!**

Heaven teaches us to be more Christlike, as described in the book of **Phil. chapter two**. It encourages us to share and put others above ourselves. Give to the poor! And if you think the poor don't matter to God, read **Psalm 12:5**.

But they (the prosperity teachers) cunningly speak against Heaven. We see the results of their teachings in 2nd Timothy 3:2: "For men will be lovers of self, (it's all about me, me, me), lovers of money, proud, arrogant, abusive, disobedient to parents ungrateful. The last part of **verse nine** says their Tongues strut through the earth. Someone will say something that sounds good, and before you know it, everyone is saying it. For instance, this phrase started with the prosperity teachers. (I'm blessed and highly favored). Some of them have no idea what they are saying. They are repeating something they heard someone else say.

Please understand this: The music industry is Satan's potent tool to capture those who are Spiritually bankrupt. Here is the sad part: **verse ten** says, "Therefore His people (God's people, - the ones who think the way of the world is better than serving God) turn and praise them; and find no fault in them. They return to this place, and waters of a full cup [offered by the wicked] are (blindly) drained by them—**verse eleven** (shows us that they are Spiritually bankrupt). And they say, "How can God know?" Is there knowledge (of us) with the Most High?"

Verse twelve: (The Spiritually bankrupt churchgoers says) "Behold, these are the wicked; always at ease, they increase in riches."

In Verse 13&14, he gives us the climax of Asaph's deceptions. Saying, "All in vain, I have cleansed my heart and washed my hands in innocence. (He's showing us how that seducing Spirit had him thinking). And he was too involved to realize God chastens whom He loves)—saying in **Verse 14**, "Because all day long, I have been stricken and chastened every morning. (He also reveals what many of our exceptionally gifted young adults, such as Asaph, are going through. They look at the Church where there are restrictions. (Which is only appealing to those who understand). Then, they look at the world where everyone is having fun, making lots of money, and doing whatever pleases them. (Which is very attractive to the flesh). So, he said in **Verse 12,** "Look, these are the wicked; always at ease, they increase in riches." (That lifestyle is very appealing)! Because of Asaph's position, the people highly respected him. In **Verse 15,** If I had said, "I will say this," [and expressed my feelings] I would have betrayed the generation of your people."

Verse sixteen (Brother Asaph confesses he was without understanding. "When I tried to understand all of this, it seemed hopeless." I will reiterate Asaph is giving us a review of his mindset while under the influence of a seducing Spirit. Because someone would think he went through all of this before coming to the house of God. Remember, David appointed him (Asaph) to oversee the music for worship. He sanged for the dedication of Solomon's temple, and he was a seer in David's court. But he said he didn't understand until he entered the Sanctuary of God.

(Take note), You can go to the house of God but never enter the Sanctuary of God. The Sanctuary of God is not a physical location but a Spiritual one. Renewing the mind helps us to align with the Spirit, who leads and guides us into all truths—making it possible to enter the Sanctuary of God. (The secret place of the Most High where we gain Spiritual insight)!.

In **Verse seventeen & eighteen**, you'll see the difference understanding makes. Saying, "Until I went into the Sanctuary of God, then I understood their end. Indeed, you set the wicked-minded and immoral on slippery places: You cast them down to destruction." How they are destroyed in a moment, swept away utterly by terror!

Verses Twenty-one & Twenty-two: He even called himself stupid. (Saying), "When I was embittered, and my innermost being was wounded, I was stupid and didn't understand. I was an unthinking animal toward you." (Understanding has truly humbled this brother). (Saying), "nevertheless, I am always with you; you hold my right hand. You guide me with your counsel, and afterward, you will take me up in glory. Who do I have in Heaven but you? And I desire nothing on earth but you. My flesh and heart may fail, but God is the strength of my heart, my portion forever."

Before Asaph finishes his discourse, he warns the ungodly. In **Verse twenty-seven:** "Those far from you will certainly perish; you destroy all who are unfaithful to you."

In **Verse twenty-eight:** (We see again how understanding has humbled this brother). When he said, [but as for me] in **Verse two**, it was in the negative tense. But look at the difference understanding has made! **Verse 28**: (But as for me, is in the positive tense). God's presence is my good. I have made the Lord my refuge, so I can tell about all you do. **(The B part of Proverbs 4:7, " In all thy getting, get an understanding").**

THE PROGRESSION OF SIN

- Sin is first pleasing; then, it proliferates. (Meaning) It increases rapidly.

- Then (Sin) it becomes delightful.

- (BECAUSE IT'S ENJOYABLE) IT'S FREQUENT.

- Then, it becomes habitual.

- Then confirmed, meaning: The man or woman is impenitent.

- Then obstinate: Not willing to change.

- Then, they resolve, never to repent, and then they are ruined.

Let's look at how sin and death entered the world. It was through the eye gates, seeing that the forbidden fruit was pleasing to the eyes. After entering the eyes, it goes to the mind, where things are assessed. Then, it goes to the heart, where things are worked or acted out.

Because we are born into sin, it becomes delightful. We all have enjoyed the pleasures of sin; that's why it becomes frequent. Then, it becomes habitual and confirmed. (Meaning) The individual is firmly established in a particular habit, belief, or way of life and is unlikely to change.

He has an impenitent heart, feeling no shame or regret about his actions or attitude. He's Obstinate, stubborn, and unwilling to change.

Then he is resolved, never repenting. His final state, he's ruined. (Brother, are you saying he can never be saved)? (NO)!

2nd Peter 3:9 Tells us, "The Lord does not delay [as though He were unable to act] and is not slow about His promises, as some count slowness, but is patient toward you, not wishing for any to perish but for all to come to repentance. **He loves us, and He doesn't want any of us to perish. That was His reason for Dying.**

THE PROGRESSIONS OF RIGHTEOUSNESS

The progressions of righteousness is a heart issue governed by Faith. First, you must believe that (GOD) exists and that He rewards those who diligently seek Him. (Which takes Faith)! Jesus said in Matthew 11:28-29, "Come unto me, all who labor and are heavy-laden, and I will give you rest. Take my yoke upon you, and learn from me; because I am meek and humble in heart, and you will find rest for souls." That means understanding who He is; you will see he's nothing like the spirit of this world. But He's meek and lowly in heart, His yoke is easy, and His burdens are light.

I have experienced the burdens and hardships of life. Knowing Him (Jesus) has given me the strength to choose what pleases the Father.

Then, you progress to putting Philippians 2:1-9 into practice. (Read it) You will see in verse 9 God rewarded Him (Jesus) for His obedience, and if you are obedient in those areas mentioned, He (The Father) will reward you also. (THEN YOU PROGRESS TO DESIRING HIM) Psalms 61:1-2 "For God alone my Soul waits for in silence: from Him (God) comes my Salvation. 2. He alone is my Rock and my Salvation, my defense, and my strong tower; I will not be shaken or disheartened.

The turbulence of life can sometimes be unbearable. But knowing Him as your Rock, you can trust Him with confidence. Psalms 62:8 says, "Trust (Confidently) in the Lord at all times, you people, pour out your heart before Him. God is a refuge for us!" David said in Psalms 16:8, "I know the Lord is always with me; I will not be shaken, for He is right beside me."

I could go on, but it takes experience to gain that kind

of confidence. If the disciples had not known or learned of Him (Jesus), they would not have had the confidence they walked with. Even to boast: saying, in Romans 5:3-5, "More than that, we rejoice in our sufferings, knowing that suffering produces endurance. Endurance produces character. Character produces hope, and hope does not disappoint us because God's Love has been poured into our hearts through the Holy Spirit, which has been given to us.

THE ISSUES OF THE HEART!

Proverbs 4:23 says, "Guard your heart with all diligence." (Why)? Because out of it (the heart) flows the issues of life. The heart is the seat of life issues, whether good or bad. (This is why God gives us a new heart)!

Many have chosen the Wide and Broadway (Which is the world), and it leads to destruction. [Satan has blinded the mind of the sinner] They don't know that he (Satan) comes to steal, kill, and destroy.

(Would you like to know why the adversary is so bold?) We must understand Satan was in Heaven! He knows how God operates. That is, he knows the system. **Ezekiel 28:1-10** Notice, in verse one, Ezekiel is referred to as the "Son of Man. God instructs him to tell the king of Tyre what will happen to him because of his pride, saying that he is a god because of his power and influence". But in **Verse 11-15,** Ezekiel said the word of the Lord came to me again. "Son of man, lament for the King of Tyre and speak to him." (But this time, THE SON OF MAN **(JESUS)** speaks directly to the adversary). "You were the signet of perfection, full of wisdom and perfect in beauty. You were in Eden, the garden of God; every precious stone was your covering: carnelian, topaz, jasper, chrysolite, carbuncle, and emerald. Their mounts and settings were worked in gold, fashioned for you the day you were created. With the cherub I placed you, I put you on the holy mountain of God. Where you walked among fiery stones. You (Satan) were blameless in your ways from the day you were created until iniquity was found in you."

Verse 15 reveals my point: He (Satan) was created by God. He was created to serve God, so God made him flawless. He was blameless in his ways from the day he was created till iniquity was found in him.

Understand this, readers: Iniquity is a nonverbal trait. It's like the fool has said in his heart: there is no God, and his behavior shows it! Take Jealousy, for instance; it's more dangerous than anger. **Proverbs 6:34** "Jealousy makes a man furious, and he will not spare when he takes revenge. He will accept no compensation. Nor be appeased through your multiple gifts. **Proverbs 27:4** Says, "Wrath is cruel, anger is overwhelming, but who can stand before Jealousy?". Those scriptures warns us of this nonverbal trait, which can be hidden, lasting, silent, subtle, violent, or an enemy often undetected until ready to do harm.

Now that we know how Satan came to be, we will look at why he is so bold. Jesus said in **Luke 10:18,** "I beheld Satan as lightning fall from Heaven." In **John 14:30,** Jesus said, "The ruler of this world comes, but he has no claim on me." **Meaning:** He (Jesus) is not of this world. So, Satan has no rule or claim on Him. But he (Satan) does have authority over this world and the unbeliever.

Isaiah 14:12, The prophet Isaiah exposed Satan's plans. Satan said, "I will ascend above the heights of the clouds; I will be **like** the **Most High**. I will imitate Him! So, he (Satan) sets up his Kingdom. The Kingdom of Darkness. A Kingdom that perverts everything God made good.

So, our Heavenly Father tells us that our adversary is the **most subtle** creature He made. **Meaning:** We are no match for him (Satan) in terms of our strength.

Our Heavenly Father has told us in advance about the adversary. So be obedient to The Father. (Why) because He loves you and wants the best for you!

(WAKE UP)!! We have an adversary who is the god of our world. He's telling us he will be like The Most High. He

(Satan) will use nonverbal traits to fulfill his purposes. The nonverbal trait God uses is Love. The nonverbal trait Satan will use is iniquity. Satan has sown iniquity in the heart of Mankind. He (Satan) knows God's attitude toward iniquity.

Therefore, God shows us the condition of the heart because of it. In **Jeremiah 17:9,** "The heart is deceitful above all things and desperately wicked: Who can know it? **Verse ten** does not leave you wondering! "I, the Lord, examine the mind; I test the heart." (Then He tells us why)! "To give to each according to his ways; according to what his actions deserve."

Proverbs 3:5: "Trust in the Lord with all your heart." **Philippians 4:19:** God said, "He would supply all of our needs according to His riches in glory." (But because sin has corrupted the heart, Satan steps in, offering false hope). Satan is telling you to strive to get riches, work hard, and follow your demonic dreams, and you can have whatever you set your mind to do.

Wake up! It is a big distraction to keep you from the truth!

Here is the truth: **Proverbs 23:4-5** "Do not labor to get rich, cease from your human wisdom." **Verse five:** "Will you set your eyes upon wealth when [suddenly] it is gone? Riches make themselves wings, like an eagle flying toward the heavens". Satan has people striving, wearing themselves out, trying to get riches. God said, stop it: decease from your human wisdom. **Proverbs 28:20** Says, "A faithful man shall abound with blessings". (Notice, He didn't say he would abound in riches, but in blessings), but he who makes haste to be rich (At any cost) shall not go unpunished.

Take heed to **1st. Timothy 6:9-10** "Those who crave to be rich fall into temptation and a snare and into many foolish (useless, godless) and hurtful desires that plunge men into ruin and destruction and miserable perishing."

Here is wisdom from our big brother (Jesus) **Luke 21:34-36:** "Take heed to yourselves and be on guard, lest your **hearts** be overburdened and depressed. (Weighed down) with the giddiness and the nausea of self-indulgence, drunkenness, and worldly worries and cares about [the business of] this life, and (lest) that day come upon you suddenly like a trap or a noose. **35.** "It will come upon all who dwell upon the whole earth." **Meaning:** No one is exempt. (If you choose that path, you will get what your actions deserve). **36.** Jesus continues, "But watch at all times, praying that you may have the **strength** to escape all these things that will take place and to stand before the Son of Man."

(Pause) Now that I understand all of this, it's funny. But it is also unfortunate because they don't know! (What's funny?) Satan causes all of this hardship; then he assigns one of his trained Pharmaceuticals to manufacture a drug to make you feel better. (What's sad?) It's unfortunate because those manufactured drugs don't change the **heart.** So people keep striving, making themselves victims. (To remind you, I'm still talking about the issues of the **heart**).

Let's take a look at Jesus's commentary on adultery. **Matt. 5:27-28**: "You have heard that it was said by them of old time, you shall not commit adultery: **28.** But I say to you, that whoever looks (nonverbal) on a woman to lust after her has already committed adultery within his **heart.**

Listen to the Spirit's commentary on hatred. **Leviticus 19:17:** "You shall not hate your brother in your **heart:** (nonverbal), but you shall surely rebuke him, lest you incur sin because of him". **1st. John 3:15** gives us a more vivid picture of hatred. "Anyone who hates his brother is a murderer, and you know that no murderer has eternal life abiding in him."

The unregenerate **heart** is full of iniquity. **Genesis 6:5** says, "The Lord saw that the wickedness of man was great in the earth and that every imagination of the thoughts of the **heart** was only evil continually."

Ecclesiastes 8:11 shows us why evil is prevailing! It says, "Because a sentence against an evil deed is not executed speedlly, man's **heart** is set to do evil.

I can accept innocence until proven guilty. But when it is blatantly apparent, execution should be done speedily - because of the depravity of men's **heart.**

GOD'S PERFECT LOVE FOR US

2nd Timothy 2:15 Does not say to read to show yourself approved. But to "Study to show yourself approved unto God!" As you do that, the Spirit of God will teach you! **1st. John 2:26-29** "I write this to you about those who would deceive you, but the anointing which you received from Him **(The Holy Spirit)** abides in you, and you have no need that anyone should teach you; as his anointing teaches you about everything and is true, and no lie, just as it has taught you, abide in him.

He can't be a God you just read about! You must remove Him from these pages and experience Him! (Many haven't experienced Him). He's our Heavenly Father! He knows us, and He wants us to know Him! He (God) knows how sin has corrupted this world: He is trying to prepare us for what is to come. Even the Apostles did what we are told to do, and that is to learn of Him. They walked with Jesus, learning from Him. They never saw Him walking in fear.

Paul gives us a declaration in **Romans 5:2,** saying, "We have also obtained access through Him (Jesus) by Faith into this grace in which we stand, and we rejoice in the hope of the glory of God. This access is a gift, enabling believers to come near Him (God) and experience His presence. Meaning we can now communicate directly to the Father through the Holy Spirit.

He, the (Spirit) will teach us everything we need to know about this life. He will lead us into all truths and convict us when we are in error.

CHILDHOOD TRAUMA

The two most harmful things a child experiences and the most common are neglect and abandonment. Let's start with neglect: Failure to care for properly. A child can have a Father and Mother in the home, but if they fail in parenting, the child suffers in the latter years.

Proverbs 29:15: "The rod and reproof give wisdom, but a child left to himself brings shame to his mother. **(Question)** Why didn't it say the child would bring shame to his parents? **(Answer)** Without the sternness of the Father, the child is left to himself, and if you fail to discipline a child when he does something wrong. That's neglect! You are training that young mind to be manipulative, and he will suffer in his later years.

Abandonment is the act of leaving someone behind or ending something permanently.

Proverbs 29:17: Discipline your son, and he will give you rest; he will give delight to your heart.

The Father is a type of **God!** He gives the rules for the home. The Wife is a type of the **Holy Spirit!** She's the helper and the nurturer. **God** and the **Holy Spirit** are in total agreement. (How)? Because they are **one!** According to scripture, The Husband and Wife are to become **one!** Nowhere in scripture will you find the **Holy Spirit** opposing **God.** That's how it should be in the home!

Then, you can apply **Proverbs 22:6** with confidence. "Train up a child in the way he should go, and when he is old, he will not depart from it."

Some of you might be saying; I know someone who was

raised in the Church. And today, he won't go near a church. I can say this with confidence! He needed to be trained by example; the headship must be **one.** When a child sees that throughout his upbringing, he will not depart from it. It's all about having a good foundation! But when children start having children, the foundation is not what it should be. (Why)? Because they are the product of neglect or abandonment. Now, we have parents killing their children and children killing their parents under the influence of a seducing Spirit. (Jesus spoke of this in **(Mark 13:12)**

Psalms 127:3-4 says, "Lo, sons are a heritage from the Lord, the fruit of the womb a reward. **4.** Like arrows in the hand of a warrior are the sons of one's youth." (RSV) The warrior wants to hit his target. We didn't have a target before coming to the knowledge of the truth. We were without understanding in this corrupt world!

But after coming to the Father through Jesus and learning of Him. We are now like arrows in the hands of our Heavenly Father. The only target set for us is to be a servant of the Most High God through our Lord and Savior, Jesus Christ. (This next topic is critical to understand).

HE'S OUR HEAVENLY FATHER

We hear many things about our Heavenly Father. But we rarely hear about how practical He is in dealing with us. Many of us are parents and we don't want our children to do wrong. But we know they do and will. We are God's children, and He doesn't want us to do wrong, but He knows we do and will. He has made it very clear in His word that He doesn't want us to sin. However, because of His love and kindness toward us, He has made provisions for us if we sin.

1st. John 1:8-10 "If we say that we have no sin, we deceive ourselves, and the truth is not in us." **9.** "If we confess our sins, He is Faithful and Just to forgive us of our sins and to cleanse us from all unrighteousness." **10.** "If we say that we have not sinned, we make him a liar, and His word is not in us." Then it goes right into **1st. John 2:1:** "My little children, these things write I unto you, that you sin not." **(Telling us He doesn't want us to sin)!** He concluded that statement by showing us His provision: saying, "If any man sin, we have an advocate with the Father, Jesus Christ the righteous:" **Verse 2.** "He is the propitiation or the atoning sacrifice for our sins, and not for ours only but also for the sins of the whole world."

One night, I ministered in a Church in Flint, Michigan, and quoted these verses from 1st. John 3:8-9 and there was a silence throughout the building. You could feel the tension - The people showed no relief until I explained the scriptures. **1st. John 3:4-10** says, "Whosoever committeth sin transgresseth also the Law: for sin is the transgression of the Law. **5.** And you know that he was manifested to take away our sins; and in Him is no sin. **6.** Whosoever abideth in him sinneth not; whosoever sinneth hath not seen Him, neither known

Him. **7.** Little children, let no man deceive you: he that doeth righteousness is righteous.

8. He that committeth sin is of the devil; for the devil sinneth from the beginning. For this purpose, the Son of God was manifested that He might destroy the works of the devil. **9.** Whosoever is born of God doth not commit sin; for His (God) seed remaineth in him: and he cannot sin, because he is born of God. **10.** In this, the children of God are manifest, and the children of the devil: whosoever doeth not righteousness is not of God, neither he that hates his brother. (Please read the rest of this chapter; it is so good for the Soul)! But I want to get to my point!

(Understanding is Key)! When you understand those scriptures, you will realize you don't have to sin. Notice, **He didn't say when you sin, but if you sin**, you have an advocate with the Father, Jesus Christ the righteous.

The Father has given us His ordinances. The Holy Spirit, the helper and nurturer. He gives us the difference between the Fruit of the Spirit and the works of the flesh. (Pause) Why the term: the works of the flesh? If you are born again, you shouldn't automatically sin, like as before. According to **2nd Cor. 5:17**, We are new creatures in Christ.

The flesh has its mind and desires. **Gal. 5:16** Says, if we walk in the Spirit, we will not fulfill the desires of the flesh. **Verse 19** gives us a list of the workings of the flesh. Then you should understand everything concerning the flesh opposes the way of the Spirit.

SIN HAS BEEN DEALT WITH

I want to show you that sin has been dealt with without getting into much history. **Hebrews 9:6-12** Reveals to us that the priest always went into the first Tabernacle, accomplishing the service of God, **Verse 7.** But into the second went the high priest alone once every year, not without blood, which he offered for himself and for the errors of the people.

Now go down to **Verse 11.** "Christ being come a high priest of good things to come, by a greater and more perfect Tabernacle, not made with hands, that is to say, not of this building." **12.** "Neither by the blood of goats and calves, but by His own blood He entered in once into the Holy place, having obtained **eternal redemption** for us."

Look also at **Hebrews 10:11-18:** "And every priest stands daily ministering and offering the same sacrifices, which can never take away sins." (Why was this priest standing daily, offering the same sacrifices for sins)? Because his works were never finished. **12.** But the Man (**Jesus),** after He had offered one sacrifice for sins forever, sat down at the right of God. (Indicating His work was finished). **14.** "For by one offering, He has perfected forever those who are sanctified." **15.** The Holy Spirit also testifies to us about this. For after He (The Holy Spirit) says: **16.** "This is the covenant I will make with them after those days", the Lord says, "I will put my laws on their hearts and write them on their minds, 17. and I will never again remember their sins and their lawless acts." 18. Where there is forgiveness of these, there is no longer any offering for sin.

Listen carefully to what Jesus said to his disciples in the 16th chapter of St. John, starting with **verse 8:** "When He the Holy Spirit comes, He will reprove or convict the world of sin, righteousness, and judgment. (I'm going to deal only with the convicting of sin). I will ask Jesus a question, and I want you to hear His answer, maybe for the first time. Jesus, "Why will the Holy Spirit convict the world of sin?" Listen to His answer: "Because they believe not in me." Notice, He didn't say, because they committed unspeakable acts of sin! But He said, "Because they believe not in me. Jesus is revealing that through the sacrifice of Himself, sin has been dealt with forever, and he is now saying come unto me, all you that labor and heavy laden, and I will give you rest. Take my yoke upon you and learn of me; because I am meek and lowly in heart; and you shall find rest unto your Souls. Because my yoke is easy, and my burden is light. **Matt. 11:28-30.**

THE SAYING IS TRUE!

Please stop and read 2nd Corinthians chapter four, which is a great reminder. But focus on **Verse 17&18:** It says, "For this slight momentary affliction is preparing for us an eternal weight of glory beyond all comparison, because we look not to the things that are seen but to the things that are unseen; For the things that are seen are temporal, but the things that are unseen are eternal."

(Take what you are about to read to heart because it is crucial to understand)! What is written is what will come to pass. We're all going to suffer at some point. We serve an invisible God, but He has revealed Himself in a way that is undeniable. So He's telling us to continue to trust in what is not seen. Because what is seen is perishing!

The Father is saying, I am the eternal one. I took on flesh and blood and became a human. I was an example, so I said learn from me. Then I suffered and died for you. Then, to prove I am God, I rosed from the dead. (**Now you know I have the victory**). I left you with promises. The major one is eternal life.

2nd Timothy 2:11-13, "The saying is sure: If we have died with him, we shall also live with Him; If we endure, we shall also reign with Him; If we deny Him, He will also deny us; If we are unfaithful, He remains Faithful because He cannot deny Himself. So avoid getting caught up in what you see because it will cause you to lose heart. Trust the invisible God and lean not to your (Human) understanding. So, it is imperative to be prayerful and a student of God's word.

We who are born again are members of His Body. And it is sad to see what politics has done to the **Body of Christ.** So, let's dismiss politics and policies and focus on character. God gave us a list of six things He hates; the seventh one is an abomination. Here are the six things God hates:

1. A haughty look.

2. A **Lying tongue.**

3. Hands that shed innocent blood.

4. A heart that devises wicked plans.

5. Feet that make haste to run to evil.

6. A false witness who breathes out lies.

7. This is the one the Father detests: **"Sowing discord among Brethren."** To sow discord among Brethren means to create or incite conflict, division, or disagreement, causing division.

Brethren typically implies a close-knit relationship, such as the Body of Christ. We are supposed to be one in Him, but look at the discord in the Church. Christians are saying they couldn't vote a certain way because of abortion and same-sex marriage.

Our Heavenly Father Gave us the ability to choose, and He will not override your will. But He will give everyone what his actions or choices deserve. Here is my point: The Government should not have power over our God-given will!

Here is a challenge: Think about how depraved you were before coming to Christ. When you read and understand **Romans 1:18-32** Read it)! You will see that God gave them over to a reprobated mind. (Why)? **Verse 26:** Because their women exchanged natural sexual relations for unnatural ones. **27.** The men, in the same way, also left natural relations with women and were inflamed in their lust for one another. Men committed shameless acts with men and received in their bodies the appropriate penalty for their error.

Here is my point: those people are of the world because they chose to follow the creature (Satan) instead of the creator (GOD). I will reiterate: you will not find a truly born-again person wanting to get an abortion or a man wanting to marry another man. Satan knows what he has done, and he continues to twist the truth.

But man can not undo what God has done! It was God who gave them over to a reprobated mind, and only by the power of the Gospel of Jesus Christ, we are delivered from the penalties of sin and corruption.

A PREVIEW OF WHAT YOU'RE GOIN TO SEE!

James 3:13-18 Who among you is wise and understanding? By his good conduct, he should show that his works are done with the gentleness that comes from wisdom. **14.** But if you have bitter envy and selfish ambition in your heart, don't boast and deny the truth. **15.** Such wisdom does not come down from above but is earthly, unspiritual, demonic. (This is what I want you to see)! **16. For where envy and selfish ambition exist, there is confusion and every evil practice. 17.** But the wisdom from above is first pure, then peaceable, gentle, open to reason, full of mercy and good fruits, without uncertainty or insincerity. If you don't, you should know that politics is of the world. (So please get this): **Colossians 1:12&13** (Please read the whole chapter to fully grasp what is being said). **12.** Giving thanks to the Father, who has qualified us to share in the inheritance of the saints in light. **13.** He has delivered us from the dominion of darkness and transferred us to the Kingdom of His Beloved Son.

People will realize God is not Republican, nor is He a Democrat. But He is a righteous God who demands justice. I hear people saying all politicians lie. That is true! Why? Because they represent the Kingdom of Darkness, and Satan is the god of that Kingdom. Some of them have morals and want to do what is right. But God has delivered us from the Kingdom of darkness and transferred us to the Kingdom of His beloved Son, Governed by God our heavenly Father.

I still find it hard to believe that Christians listened to this man lie every time he opened his mouth. The whole world saw what he did, and he is still lying. The word of God was given to us to live by, to show that we are of the Kingdom of light! But some have blatantly ignored the warning.

Here is the warning: Isaiah 5:20 Says, "Woe to those who call evil good, and good evil; who put darkness for light, and light for darkness: who put bitter for sweet and sweet for bitter! This verse warns against the dangers of losing sight of true moral principles and inverting God's standard of right and wrong.

I believe God revealed hearts in this last election, which has nothing to do with policies but character. Yes, it was a she and not a he, but what came out of her mouth was closer to the heart of God—helping the poor, protecting our social security, and giving aid to the unfortunate.

Oppose to someone talking about getting revenge on people he claimed did him wrong. We who are born-again have been delivered from the Kingdom of darkness. But if you get involved, choose what is pure, peaceable, gentle, and open to reason. Full of mercy and good fruits.

Everyone knows that number forty-seven has selfish ambition, and everything that came out of his mouth was earthly, unspiritual, demonic. Brother James tells us what we will experience under someone with selfish ambition, which is confusion and every evil practice.

James 3:17: "But the wisdom from above is first pure, then peaceable, gentle, open to reason, full of mercy and good fruits, without uncertainty or insincerity. Look at the uncertainty we are faced with daily.

I genuinely feel sorry for those who don't understand because **UNDERSTANDING IS KEY!** Please understand me. There is so much I don't understand. But what I know came from studying, praying, and, most importantly, experience.

YOU MUST BE BORN-AGAIN

To give you a clear picture, I will explain why you must be born again, starting from the Old Testament. The Old Testament is pictorial, which is something expressed in a picture or make a picture for mind. Reading Genesis gives us a picture of what happened in the Garden of Eden.

I want to clarify that I am not disregarding what is written because there are many applications and principles of faith as to how God created the world by the power of His Word.

My reason for addressing this is: I would hear people making statements, "saying if it weren't for Adam, we wouldn't be in all of this mess. There's something about that statement that doesn't add up. Because indirectly, they are saying that Jesus was God's alternant plan, you know, just in case Adam fails. We can always count on Jesus!

They make it sound as if Adam hadn't sinned, he would have reached some kind of spiritual utopia. You wouldn't make statements like that when you understand that God never intended for righteousness to come through Adam. Revelations Chapter 13:8 says, "Jesus was the Lamb slain before the foundation of the world. Therefore, His suffering for the Salvation of Mankind was foreordained or decided long before Adam was formed.

Ist. Cor. 15:45-49, The Holy Spirit clearly distinguishes between the first Adam and the second Adam. Let's look at them.

1. The first Adam was a living Soul.

2. The second Adam was made a quickening or life-giving Spirit.

3. The first Adam was natural. The second Adam was Spiritual.

4. The first Adam was earthy. The second Adam was Heavenly.

I will also suggest to you that the first Adam was carnal, natural, or unspiritual before sinning. In Genesis 2:16, God Commanded this natural man not to eat from the tree of the knowledge of good and evil. Genesis 3:6-7 shows that this command was disobeyed, and we see the consequence: death.

In Romans 5:12-13, Paul explains, "By one man sin entered into the world, and death by sin; and so death passed upon all men, because of that all have sinned. So everything about this natural man agrees with the world system. That's why it is so easy to be induced by sin.

Then, after God judges him, He (God) has to make him aware of sin. Ver. 13 says, "For until the Law, sin was in the world: but sin is not imputed when there is no law. Verse 14 says, "Nevertheless death reigned from Adam to Moses, even over them that had not sinned after the similitude of Adam's transgression, who is the figure of Him (Jesus) was to come. (Question) Why did death reign from Adam to Moses? (Answer) Because Moses was the Lawgiver. The Law brought death to a halt; It didn't abolish death. (Why)? Because God never intended for righteousness to come by way of the Law.

Look at the (B) part of Gal.3:21, which says, "If there had been a Law given which could have given life, truly righteousness should have been by the Law. Ver.22 "But the scripture has concluded all under sin, that the promise by faith in Jesus Christ might be given to them that believe. Ver. 23 "But before faith came, we were kept under the Law, shut up unto the faith which should afterwards be revealed." We see in verse 24 that the Law was our schoolmaster to bring us unto Christ, that we might be Justified by faith. The Law was only a temporary provision to show sinners their need for grace.

Understand this also, that man couldn't keep the Ten Commandments. (Why)? The first nine were Objective, which is based on facts. It can be something we try to accomplish by our efforts. The tenth one is subjective and deals with our feelings, thoughts, and experiences. We can say I haven't committed adultery, or I haven't killed or did this or that. But number ten says, "Thou shall not covet, " which messed up everything.

In Matt. 5:28 Jesus said, "If you look at a woman to lust after her, you have already committed adultery with her in your heart. Romans 7:7-8, we see that the tenth command-ment caused Paul to see all kinds of evil desires that he would not have seen apart from the Law. So, the Law ful-filled its purpose.

But righteousness would come by one: Jesus Christ! Ac-cording to the (B) part of 1st. Cor. 15:49: "We shall also bear His Image. Romans 8:29 says, "For whom He did foreknow, (that will be us) He also did predestinate to be conformed to the image of His Son. Also, the adoption was predestinat-ed according to the good pleasure of His will by Jesus Christ Himself.

The word predestinate means to determined before-hand. So, this was fixed in God's plains for man. We must stop looking at the negative aspects of what the first Adam did and see what God did according to His purpose. God was not surprised when Adam sinned. (Some of you might say), Then why did God ask them, "What have you done? (I ex-plained that in full in THE TRUTH THE REVISED VERSION un-der the topic Adam and Eve).

Heb. 1:1-2 "Long ago God spoke to the fathers by the

prophets at different times and in different ways. 2. In these last days, He has spoken to us by his Son." The Son has spoken, and the most essential words He revealed to man are in St. John 3:3-7 He said, "Except a man be born again, he cannot see the Kingdom of God. 4. Nicodemus says to Him, how can a man be born when is old? Can he enter into his mother's womb the second time and be born? 5. Jeusu answered, "Truly, truly, I say unto you, except a man be born of water and of the Spirit, he cannot enter the Kingdom of God." 6. "That which is born of the flesh is flesh, and that which born of the Spirit is Spirit." 7. " Marvel not that I said you must be BORN-AGAIN."

Everyone that is born is born of the flesh. Now, you must be born-again of the Spirit and begin renewing your mind with God's Word. Because His Word is Spirit and it's Life.

May God bless and keep you, and remember, he who loves is born of God. Because God is Love!

"If this book is a blessing to you feel free to give an offering"